The DRESSER

by RONALD HARWOOD

SAMUEL FRENCH, INC.

45 WEST 25TH STREET   NEW YORK 10010
7623 SUNSET BOULEVARD HOLLYWOOD 90046
LONDON   TORONTO

The Dresser was first performed at the Royal Exchange Theatre, Manchester on 6 March 1980 with the following cast:

NORMAN	*Tom Courtenay*
HER LADYSHIP	*Isabel Dean*
IRENE	*Jacqueline Tong*
MADGE	*Carol Gillies*
SIR	*Freddie Jones*
GEOFFREY THORNTON	*Lockwood West*
MR OXENBY	*Geoffrey McGivern*

Players in *King Lear*

GLOUCESTER	*Rex Arundel*
KNIGHT	
ALBANY	
	Anthony Benson
KNIGHT	
	Joe Holmes
GENTLEMAN	
KENT	*Guy Nicholls*

Directed by Michael Elliott
Set designed by Laurie Dennett
Costumes designed by Stephen Doncaster
Lighting by Mark Henderson
Sound by Ian Gibson

The play was presented at the Queen's Theatre, London on 30 April 1980 by Michael Codron with the following change of cast:

HER LADYSHIP	*Jane Wenham*
MADGE	*Janet Henfrey*
KNIGHT	
	Peter O'Dwyer
GENTLEMAN	
KNIGHT	
	Kenneth Oxtoby
ALBANY	
KENT	*David Browning*
ELECTRICIAN	*Trevor Griffiths*

BROOKS ATKINSON THEATRE

UNDER THE DIRECTION OF THE MESSRS. NEDERLANDER

JAMES M. NEDERLANDER   ELIZABETH I. McCANN   NELLE NUGENT
WARNER THEATRE PRODUCTIONS INC.
and MICHAEL CODRON
present

TOM COURTENAY PAUL ROGERS

in

The DRESSER

by RONALD HARWOOD

with

RACHEL GURNEY

| LISABETH | DON McALLEN | MARGE | DOUGLAS |
| BARTLETT | LESLIE | REDMOND | SEALE |

| LESLIE | JEFFREY ALAN | JEROME | RICHARD | GEOFF |
| BARRETT | CHANDLER | COLLAMORE | FRANK | GARLAND |

| Sets by | Costumes by | Lighting by | Sound by |
| LAURIE DENNETT | STEPHEN DONCASTER | BEVERLY EMMONS | IAN GIBSON |

| Sets Supervision by | Costumes Supervision by | Sound Supervision by |
| KAREN SCHULZ | JEANNE BUTTON | T. RICHARD FITZGERALD |

Directed by
MICHAEL ELLIOTT

The Dresser was first produced at the Royal Exchange Theatre, Manchester.
It was produced at the Queen's Theatre, London by Michael Codron.

CAST

(in order of appearance)

Norman	TOM COURTENAY
Her Ladyship	RACHEL GURNEY
Madge	MARGE REDMOND
Sir	PAUL ROGERS
Irene	LISABETH BARTLETT
Geoffrey	DOUGLAS SEALE
Oxenby	DON McALLEN LESLIE
Electrician	GEOFF GARLAND
Kent	JEFFREY ALAN CHANDLER
Gloucester	LESLIE BARRETT
Gentleman	RICHARD FRANK
Knight 1	JEROME COLLAMORE
Knight 2	RICHARD FRANK
Albany	JEROME COLLAMORE

The play is set in January 1942 in a theatre in the English provinces.

ACT I
Before curtain up.

ACT II
After curtain up.

Characters

NORMAN

HER LADYSHIP

MADGE

SIR

IRENE

GEOFFREY THORNTON

MR OXENBY

Two Knights, Gloucester, Kent.

January 1942. A theatre in the English provinces.

Act I: Before curtain-up.

Act II: After curtain-up.

THE DRESSER

ACT I

SIR's *dressing room and corridor. Sound of air raid siren, and AIR RAID WARDEN's VOICE calling for 'Lights out' and 'There's an air-raid on, the air-raid warning's gone!' etc. A radio is on giving news of the war, Mr. Churchill etc. Light on* NORMAN, *who is ironing, listening to the news. Light grows to reveal a mud-stained overcoat and crumpled Homburg lying on the floor. Footsteps.* NORMAN *becomes alert.* HE *rises.* HER LADYSHIP *enters.* SHE *stands just inside the doorway.* NORMAN *turns off the radio.*

HER LADYSHIP. He does nothing but cry.

NORMAN. Are they keeping him in?

HER LADYSHIP. They wouldn't let me stay. The doctor said I seemed to make matters worse.

NORMAN. I shouldn't have taken him to the hospital. I don't know what came over me. I should have brought him back here where he belongs.

HER LADYSHIP. Why is his coat on the floor? And his hat—?

NORMAN. Drying out. They're wet through, sodden, if you don't mind my saying so. So was he. Drenched. Sweat and drizzle—

7

HER LADYSHIP. How did he come to be in such a state, Norman? When you telephoned, I thought at first he'd been hurt in the air raid—

NORMAN. No—

HER LADYSHIP. Or had an accident—

NORMAN. No, not an accident—

HER LADYSHIP. No, I know because they said there was no sign of physical injury—

NORMAN. Your ladyship—

HER LADYSHIP. He's in a state of collapse—

NORMAN. I know—

HER LADYSHIP. How did he get like that?

NORMAN. Your ladyship—

HER LADYSHIP. What happened to him?

NORMAN. Sit down. Please. Please, sit down. (SHE *does so*) We have to remain calm, not to say clear-headed.

HER LADYSHIP. The doctor said it must have been coming on for weeks.

NORMAN. If not longer.

HER LADYSHIP. I didn't see him this morning. He left the digs before I woke. Where was he all day? Where did you find him?

NORMAN. What happened was this, your ladyship: after the last 'All-clear' sounded I went into Market Square as dusk was coming on, a peculiar light, ever so yellowish, smoke and dust rising from the bomb craters, running shadows, full of the unexpected. I had hoped to find a packet or two of Brown and Polson's cornflour since our supplies are rather low and the stuff's scarce and you never know. So I was asking at this stall and that when I heard his voice.

HER LADYSHIP. Whose voice?

NORMAN. Sir's, of course. I turned and saw him by the candle-maker who was shutting up shop for the night. He was lit by one tall tallow candle which was guttering and he looked like that painting of him as Lear, all greens and dark blues seen through this peculiar light. He was taking off his overcoat, in this weather. "God help the man who stops me," he shouted, and threw the coat to the ground just like Lear in the storm scene. Look at it. I don't know if I'll ever get it clean. And he was so proud of it, do you remember or perhaps it was before your time? The first Canadian tour, Toronto, Raglan sleeves, fur collar, and now look at it.

HER LADYSHIP. What happened after he took off his coat?

NORMAN. Started on the hat. Dunn's Piccadilly, only a year ago, down on the coat it went and he jumped on it, stamped on his hat, viciously stamped on his hat. You can see. He lifted both hands as he does to convey sterility into Goneril's womb and called out, "How much further do you want me to go?" His fingers were all of a fidget, undoing his jacket, loosening his collar and tie, tearing at the buttons of his shirt.

HER LADYSHIP. Were there many people about?

NORMAN. A small crowd. That's why I ran to him.

HER LADYSHIP. Did he know who you were?

NORMAN. I didn't wait to find out. I just took his hand and said, "Good evening, Sir, shouldn't we be getting to the theatre?" in my best nanny-voice, the one I use when he's being wayward. He paid no attention. He was shivering. His whole body seemed to be trembling, and such a trembling.

HER LADYSHIP. You shouldn't have let the public see him like that.

NORMAN. I tried to spirit him away, only just then, a woman approached, quite old, wearing bombazine under a tweed coat but perfectly respectable. She'd picked up his clothes and wanted to help him dress. I just stood there, amazed, utterly amazed. He said to the woman, "Thank you my dear, but Norman usually looks after me. I'd be lost without Norman," so I thought to myself this is your cue, ducky, and said "I'm Norman, I'm his dresser." The woman—she had her hair in curlers—took his hand and kissed it, saying, "You were lovely in *The Corsican Brothers*." He looked at her a long while, smiled sweetly, you know the way he does when he's wanting to charm, and said, "Thank you, my dear, but you must excuse me. I have to make an exit," and ran off.

HER LADYSHIP. He said, I have to make an exit?

NORMAN. Well, of course, I went after him, fearing the worst. I didn't know he could run so fast. I just followed a trail of discarded clothing, jacket, waistcoat, and thought we can't have Sir doing a striptease round the town. But then I found him. Leaning up against a lamp-post. Weeping. Without a word, hardly knowing what I was doing, I led him to the hospital. The Sister didn't recognise him, although later she said she'd seen him as Othello last night. A doctor was summoned, short, bald, bespectacled, and I was excluded by the drawing of screens.

HER LADYSHIP. And then you telephoned me.

NORMAN. No. I waited. I lurked, as Edmund says, and heard the doctor whisper, "This man is exhausted. This man is in a state of collapse." Then the Sister came out and said I must fetch you at once. That's when I telephoned. And that's how it happened. (*Pause. 'All-clear' sounds*) There goes the 'All-clear.'

HER LADYSHIP. What are we to do? In just over an hour there'll be an audience in this theatre hoping to see him as King Lear. What am I to do?

NORMAN. Don't upset yourself for a start.

HER LADYSHIP. I've never had to make this sort of decision before. Any sort of decision before. This morning, our landlady reported something. After breakfast, while I was still asleep, he sat at the dining table writing, she said, or trying to write, but all he did was to crumple up sheet after sheet of paper. When I came down I smoothed them out to see what he'd written. My Life. My Life. The rest of the page was empty.

NORMAN. He said to me his autobiography would be his only memorial. "Have you written much," I asked? "Not a word," he said. And last night, after *Othello,* he asked me, "What do we play tomorrow, Norman?" I told him *King Lear* and he said, "Then I shall wake with the storm clouds in my head."

HER LADYSHIP. I should have made him rest. The doctor said he'd come to the end of his rope and found it frayed.

NORMAN. You should've told the doctor all about the troubles—

HER LADYSHIP. No. Civilians never understand.

NORMAN. That's true. Doctors. Just imagine trying to explain to a doctor what Sir's been through. "Well, you see, doctor, he's been trying to recruit actors for his Shakespearean company but all the able-bodied and best ones are in uniform, and the theatres are bombed to bits as soon as you book them, not to mention the trouble this week with Mr. Davenport-Scott." Doctors. He'd have had his hypodermic rampant before you could say 'As You Like It'. That's all they know. Hypodermics.

HER LADYSHIP. What's the latest on Mr. Davenport-Scott?

NORMAN. If you don't mind, I'd rather not discuss Mr. Davenport-Scott with a lady. I'll tell Madge all about it when she comes in. Suffice to say he will not be making an appearance this evening.

(*Pause*)

HER LADYSHIP. There's no alternative. We'll have to cancel.

NORMAN. Oh no, your ladyship, cancellation's ever so drastic.

HER LADYSHIP. He's ill. There's no crime in being ill, it's not high treason, not a capital offence, not desertion in the face of the enemy. He's not himself. He can work. Will the world stop turning? Will the Nazis overrun England? One Lear more or less in the world won't make any difference.

NORMAN. Sir always believes it will.

HER LADYSHIP. Who really cares whether he acts or not?

NORMAN. There's bound to be someone.

(*Pause*)

HER LADYSHIP. I never imagined it would end like this. I've always thought he was indestructible.

NORMAN. This'll be the first time we've ever cancelled. I want to go to the hospital—

HER LADYSHIP. No, Norman—

NORMAN. I want to sit with him and be with him and try to give him comfort. I can usually make him smile. Perhaps when he sees me—

HER LADYSHIP. They wouldn't even let me stay.

(NORMAN *fights tears. Pause*)

NOGMAN. Sixteen years. I wish I could remember the name of the girl who got me into all this. Motherly type she was, small parts, play as cast. I can see her face clearly. I can see her standing there, Platform 2 at Crewe. A Sunday. I was on Platform 4. "Norman," she called. We'd been together in *Outward Bound*, the Number Three tour, helped with wardrobe I did, understudied Scrubby, the steward. That's all aboard a ship, you know. Lovely first act. "We're all dead, aren't we?" And I say, "Yes, Sir, we're all dead. Quite dead." And he says, "How long have you been—you been—oh you know?" "Me, Sir? Oh, I was lost young." And he says, "Where— where are we sailing for?" And I say, "Heaven, Sir. And hell, too. It's the same place, you see." Lovely. Anyway. "Norman!" she called. What was her name? She'd joined Sir, oh, very hoity-toity, I thought, tiaras and blank verse while I was in panto understudying the Ugly Sisters. Both of them.

"Are you fixed?" she shouted at the top of her voice. Well. To cut a short story shorter, Sir wanted help in the wardrobe and someone to assist generally, but mainly with the storm in *Lear*. I've told you this before, haven't I? Put me on the timpani, he did. On the first night, after the storm, while he was waiting to go on for 'No, you cannot touch me for coining', he called me over. My knees were jelly. "Where you on the timpani tonight?" "Yes, sir," I said, fearing the worst. "Thank you," he said. "You're an artist." I didn't sleep a wink. Next day he asked if I'd be his dresser. (*Pause*) Madge. You can always tell. She walks as if the band were playing Onward Christian Soldiers.

(MADGE *knocks on dressing room door and goes in*)

MADGE. Any further developments?

(HER LADSHIP *shakes her head*)

MADGE. We had better see the manager. Perhaps you ought to come with me.

NORMAN. Oh, your ladyship, please, let's take our time, let's not rush things—

MADGE. (*To* HER LADYSHIP) There's no alternative.

HER LADYSHIP. Madge is right, he's in hospital. We can't play *King Lear* without the King. We have to made a decision.

NORMAN. Forgive me, your ladyship, it's not a decision you have to make, it's the right decision. I had a friend, before one's face was lined, as the saying goes, in a very low state he was, ever so fragile, a pain to be with. You weren't safe from

him on top of a bus. If he happened to sit beside
you, he'd tell you the ABC of unhappiness between
bus stops. Someone close to him, his mother, I believe,
though it was never proved, understandably upset,
made a decision. A little rest, she said, among those
similarly off-centre, in Colwyn Bay, never a good
date, not in February, wrapped in a grey rug, gazing
at a grey sea. Talk about bleak. Mother-dear made
a decision but it was the wrong decision. My friend
never acted again.

MADGE. (*To* HER LADYSHIP) We have to face the
facts.

NORMAN. I've never done that in my life, your
ladyship, and I don't see why I should start now.
I just like things to be lovely. No pain, that's my
motto.

MADGE. But things aren't lovely, Norman.

NORMAN. They aren't if you face facts. Face the
facts, it's facing the company I worry about. Poor
lambs. What'll happen to them? And the customers?
There was a line at the box office this afternoon,
if four elderly spinsters constitute a line. Pity to
give them their money back, they've likely had enough
disappointment in life as it is. It's no good Sir talking
about responsibility and service and struggle and
survival and then you go and cancel the performance.

MADGE. (*To* HER LADYSHIP) It's a disease.

HER LADYSHIP. What is?

MADGE. Hopefulness. I think we should discuss this
in private. I'll be in my room. (SHE *goes.* HER LADY-
SHIP *is about to follow.*)

HER LADYSHIP. Years ago, in my father's Shakespearean company. he unmTentionable Scots tragedy. A
new Macduff. Couldn't remember the lines. My father

should've sacked him at the end of the first rehearsal. But no, my father said, "He'll know it." He never did.

NORMAN. Oh well, that was the Scots tragedy. Everyone knows that's the unluckiest play in the world. That's the one superstition I believe in absolutely. That play would turn a good fairy wicked.

HER LADYSHIP. In the fight scene. The man couldn't remember the fight. He thrust when he shouldn't have and sliced my father's face across. The right cheek seized up in a lopsided grin. The only part left to my father was Caliban.

NORMAN. It's not the same thing—

HER LADYSHIP. I'll be in Madge's room if I'm wanted.

NORMAN. Don't decide yet, your ladyship, let me go to the hospital, let me see how he is, you never know—

HER LADYSHIP. I do know. I realise now I've witnessed a slow running-down. I've heard the hiss of air escaping. We'll call the company together at the half. I'll tell them—

(NORMAN *is suddenly alert*)

HER LADYSHIP. —that tonight's performance is cancelled, that the engagement is to be ended—

(*Heavy footsteps.* BOTH *look at each other. Footsteps nearer.* SIR *enters in a dishevelled state. Long pause.*)

NORMAN. Good evening, Sir.

SIR. Good evening, Norman. Good evening, Pussy.

HER LADYSHIP. Bonzo, why are you here?

SIR. My name is on the door.

HER LADYSHIP. Did the doctors say you could leave?

SIR. Doctors? Executioners. Do you know what he told me? A short, bald butcher, *Il Duce* in a white coat. "You need rest," he said. Is that all? When a doctor tells you you need rest, you can be certain he hasn't the slightest idea of what's wrong with you. I discharged myself. (HE *weeps*)

HER LADYSHIP. (*To* NORMAN) Telephone the hospital.

SIR. Do not telephone the hospital. (HE *continues to weep*)

HER LADYSHIP. Norman, will you leave us; please?

NORMAN. I'll see Madge and tell her there's an alternative. (NORMAN *goes. Silence*)

HER LADYSHIP. (*With real disgust*) You're fit for nothing.

SIR. Please, Pussy, don't.

HER LADYSHIP. Cancel the performance.

SIR. Can't. Mustn't. Won't.

HER LADYSHIP. Then take the consequences.

SIR. When have I not?

HER LADYSHIP. The doctor promised you'd be kept there.

SIR. They tried to inject me. They couldn't hold me down.

HER LADYSHIP. Where have you been all day? Don't tell me you found a brothel in this town.

SIR. I can't remember all I've done. I know towards evening I was being pursued but I couldn't see who the villains were. Then the warning went.

I refused to take shelter. I'm accustomed to the blasted heath. Acrid smell. Eyes watering. Wherever I went I seemed to hear a woman crying. Suddenly, I had a clear image of my father on the beach near Lowestoft, plans in his hands, inspecting the boats his men had built. "An actor?" he said, "Never. You will be a boat builder like me." But I defied him and lost his love. Father preferred people to cower. But I had to chart my own course. I decide when I'm ready for the scrap-yard. Not you. I and no one else. I. (HE *sits and stares*)

HER LADYSHIP. The woman you heard crying was me.

SIR. (*Calling*) Norman! Norman! Norman!

(NORMAN *comes running down the corridor and goes into the dressing room, followed shortly by* MADGE)

NORMAN. Sir.

SIR. Norman, I want you by me.

NORMAN. Yes, Sir.

SIR. Don't leave my side, Norman.

NORMAN. No, Sir.

SIR. I shall want help, Norman.

NORMAN. Yes, Sir.

(MADGE *knocks and enters*)

SIR. Madge-dear.

HER LADYSHIP. (*To* MADGE) You speak to him. He doesn't hear a word I say. He's obviously incapable—

MADGE. (*To* SIR) You look exhausted.

NORMAN. That's what I call tact.

MADGE. Are you sure you're able to go on tonight?

NORMAN. He wouldn't be here if he wasn't, would you, Sir?

SIR. (*To* MADGE) How long have you been with me, Madge-dear?

MADGE. Longer than anyone else.

SIR. How long?

MADGE. Twenty years, nearly twenty years.

SIR. Have I ever missed a performance?

MADGE. No, but then you've never been ill.

(SIR *sits and stares*)

MADGE. (*Quietly*) I only want what's best for you.

NORMAN. What's best for Sir is that he's allowed to get ready.

SIR. Ready, yes, I must get ready. (HE *waves them away*)

MADGE. Ready for what? (SHE *goes*. SIR *sits and stares*)

NORMAN. Excuse me, your ladyship, shouldn't you be getting ready, too? (HE *puts a kettle on a small gas ring*)

HER LADYSHIP. I can't bear to see him like that.

NORMAN. Then best to leave us. I've had experience of these things. I know what has to be done.

(SIR *stifles a sob*)

HER LADYSHIP. Imagine waking to that night after night. (SHE *goes*. NORMAN *secretly takes a quarter*

bottle of brandy from his pocket and has a swig.
HE *replaces the bottle and turns to* SIR)

NORMAN. Right! Shall we begin at the beginning?
(*Pause*) Good evening, Sir. (*Pause*) Good evening,
Norman. And how are you this evening, Sir? A
little tearful, I'm afraid, and you, Norman? I'm
very well, thank you, Sir, had ever such a quiet
day, cleaning your wig and beard, ironing your
costumes, washing your undies. And what have you
been up to, Sir? I've been jumping on my hat,
Norman. Have you? That's an odd thing to do.
May one ask why? Why what, Norman? Why we've
been jumping on our hat, Sir? Not much fun for
me this conversation, not much fun for you either,
I suspect. (*Pause*) Are we going to sulk all evening,
or are we going to speak to our servants? (*Pause*)
I do wish you'd stop crying, Sir. (*Pause*) Shall
we play 'I Spy'? I spy with my little eye something
beginning with A. I know you won't guess so I'll
tell. A is for actor. And actors have to work, and
actors have to put on their make-up and change
their frocks and then, of course, actors have to
act. Zounds, madam, where dost thou get this knowledge? From a baboon, Sir, that wandered wild
in Eden. Or words to that effect. I've never known
a kettle take so long to boil. Tell you what, have
a little brandy. Break the rules, have a nip. A
little brandy won't harm as the surgeon said to
the undertaker's widow.

(*No response.* NORMAN *has a nip of brandy himself*)

NORMAN. There's less than an hour to go. You
usually want longer. Shall we make a start?

SIR *looks up at him*)

NORMAN. Yes, it's me, Norman, the one with
the soulful eyes. (*The kettle boils.* NORMAN *makes
tea*) I saved my rations for you. I don't mind going
without. (HE *hums to himself and then takes a cup
to* SIR) Drink up. It's tea, not rat poison. (NORMAN
sits beside SIR *and feeds him the tea.* SIR *drinks
tea*) There. That's better, isn't it? Isn't it? (SIR
moistens his lips) Would you like a bicky? I saved
one from the mayor's reception in Bridlington. No?
Then why don't you have one, Norman? Thanks
very much, I will. (HE *takes a biscuit from the
tin and eats it*) If you don't mind my saying so,
Sir, there seems little point in discharging yourself
from hospital, and coming to sit here like Niobe
prior to being turned into stone. So. Shall we make
an effort? (SIR *tries to loosen his collar and tie*)
Let me. That's what I'm here for. (HE *helps* SIR,
who suddenly grabs hold of NORMAN, *buries his
face in his neck and sobs*) I know how it feels.
I had a friend, worse than you he was, and all
they ever wanted to do with him was put him away.
And no one wants to go through that. Or so my
friend said. They'll send you to Colwyn Bay and
you know you never do any business in Colwyn
Bay. And guess what got my friend well? Sounds
silly this. An offer of work. A telegram, yes, fancy,
a telegram. Can you understudy Scrubby *Outward
Bound* start Monday? He discharged himself, just
like you, my friend did, took the train up to London,
found digs in Brixton and never looked back. What
do you make of that? An offer of work. Meant

someone had thought of him and that's ever such a comfort. (SIR *disengages himself*) So here's something to cheer you up. It's going to be a Full House tonight. All those people thinking of you and wanting you to act.

(*Long pause*)

  SIR. Really? A Full House?
  NORMAN. Shall we make a start?

(*Long pause*)

  SIR. What play is it tonight?
  NORMAN. *King Lear*, Sir.
  SIR. Impossible.
  NORMAN. Thank you very much, that's nice, isn't it? People paying good money to see you and you say impossible, very nice indeed, I don't think.

(*Pause*)

  SIR. I don't want to be seen.
  NORMAN. Difficult when you're playing King Lear with the lighting you use.
  SIR. I don't want to see Her Ladyship.
  NORMAN. Even more difficult since she's playing Cordelia. You saw her a moment ago. You were alone together.
  SIR. Were we? What's the play tonight?
  NORMAN. *King Lear*, Sir.

(*Pause*)

SIR. Madge was wrong.

NORMAN. She often is.

SIR. I have been ill before. Did you ever see me in *The Corsican Brothers*?

NORMAN. Alas no, Sir, before my time.

SIR. I went on with double pneumonia. Apt when you're playing the Corsican Brothers. I'd rather have double pneumonia than this.

NORMAN. Than what?

(SIR *allows* NORMAN *to help him undress*)

SIR. What prevents me from packing up and going home? Why am I here when I should be asleep? Even kings abdicate.

NORMAN. Well I hope he's happy with the woman he loves, that's all I can say, I hope he's happy. Shall we undress? Talk of undressing, wasn't it a strange light in Market Square this evening?

SIR. I don't remember being in Market Square.

NORMAN. You've been missing the whole day. What do you remember?

SIR. Walking, walking, walking. If only I could find a good, catchy title. I think *My Life* a little plain, don't you?

NORMAN. Still stuck, are we?

SIR. No. I wrote a little today. Two or three sides of an exercise book. But I can't find a title.

NORMAN. We'll think of something.

SIR. See if it's still in my coat. And my reading glasses.

(NORMAN *looks in the pocket of the overcoat, finds*

the exercise book and a pair of broken spectacles.
HE *takes the book to* SIR *and holds up the
spectacles*)

NORMAN. You won't see much through these.

(SIR *pages through the book*)

SIR. I thought I'd written today. Look for me.
Is there anything?

(NORMAN *flicks through the pages*)

SIR. No. Evidently not. It can't be *Lear* again?
NORMAN. Shall we begin our makeup? (HE *guides*
SIR *to the dressing table but* SIR *stops suddenly*)

SIR. Where's my hat? I'm getting out of here.
I'm not staying in this place a moment longer.
I'm surrounded by vipers, betrayal on every side.
I am being crushed, the life blood is draining out
of me. The load is too great. Norman, Norman,
if you have any regard for me, don't listen to him—
NORMAN. Who? Who?

SIR. More, more, more, I can't give any more,
I have nothing more to give. I want a tranquil senility.
I'm a grown man. I don't want to go on painting
my face night after night, wearing clothes that are
not my own, I'm not a child dressing up for charades,
this is my work, my life's work, I'm an actor,
and who cares if I go out there tonight or any
other night and shorten my life? (HE *sits, buries
his face in his hands*)

NORMAN. I had a friend once said, "Norman,

I don't care if there are only three people out front,
or if the audience laugh when they shouldn't, or
don't when they should, one person, just one person
is certain to know and understand. And I act for
him." That's what my friend said.

SIR. I can't move that which can't be moved.

NORMAN. What are we on about now?

SIR. I'm filled inside with stone. Stone upon stone.
I can't lift myself. The weight is too much. I know
futility when I see it. I dream at night of unseen
hands driving wooden stakes into my feet. I can't
move, and when I look at the wounds I see a
jellied, leprous pus. And the dream is long and
graceless. I wake up, sweat-drenched, poisoned. And
the whole day long there is a burning heat inside
me, driving all else from my mind. What did I
do today?

NORMAN. You walked. You thought you wrote.
You were in Market Square. A woman kissed your
hand and said you were lovely in *The Corsican
Brothers*.

SIR. How do you know all this? Has someone
been talking?

(Pause)

NORMAN. I don't wish to hurry you, Sir, no, I
lie, I do.

SIR. I hate the swines.

NORMAN. Who?

SIR. He's a hard task-master, he drives me too
hard. I have too much to carry.

(MADGE *knocks on the door.* NORMAN *opens it but doesn't admit her*)

NORMAN. Yes?

MADGE. I'd like to see him.

NORMAN. I'd rather you didn't.

MADGE. It's my responsibility to take the curtain up tonight. There isn't much time.

NORMAN. Things have reached a delicate stage. I don't want him disturbed.

SIR. What's all the whispering?

NORMAN. Nothing, nothing.

MADGE. Has he begun to make up yet?

NORMAN. Not yet but—

MADGE. Do you realise how late it is? They'll be calling the half in a moment.

NORMAN. I know how late it is.

MADGE. Then on your head be it. (SHE *goes*)

SIR. Who was that?

NORMAN. Only Madge to say everything's running like clockwork. (HE *looks anxiously at his watch*) Oh, look! A dressing-gown! Shall we put it on and keep ourselves warm? (HE *helps* SIR *on with his dressing-gown*) What's it matter where you were or what you did today? You're here, in the theatre, safe and sound, where you belong. And a Full House. Lovely.

SIR. Really? A Full House?

NORMAN. There'll be standing room only. (NORMAN *guides* SIR *to the dressing table.* SIR *sits and stares at himself in the looking-glass*)

SIR. Do you know they bombed the Grand Theatre, Plymouth?

NORMAN. And much else of the city besides.

SIR. I made my debut at the Grand Theatre, Plymouth.

NORMAN. They weren't to know.

SIR. I shouldn't have come out this autumn, but I had no choice. He made me.

NORMAN. Who?

SIR. I should have rested.

NORMAN. I had a friend who was ordered to rest. He obeyed. That was the end of him. He was ever so ill. Nearly became a Catholic. (*Pause*) Would you like a little rub-down? (*No response*) I'm not surprised you're feeling dispirited. It's been ever such a hard time. No young men to play the juveniles and the trouble with Mr. Davenport-Scott.

(SIR *is suddenly alert*)

SIR. What news of Mr. Davenport-Scott?

NORMAN. The police have opposed bail.

SIR. What?

NORMAN. Well, he'd had his second warning.

SIR. How then do we dispose our forces?

NORMAN. Mr. Thornton is standing by to play Fool.

SIR. And who as Oswald?

NORMAN. Mr Browne, I'm afraid.

SIR. That leaves me a Knight short for 'Reason not the need'.

NORMAN. Ninety-eight short, actually, if you take the text as gospel, so one more or less won't be too upsetting.

SIR. Thornton toothless as Fool. Browne lisping

as Oswald. Oxenby limping as Edmund. What have I come to? I've never had a company like this one. I'm reduced to old men, cripples and nancy-boys. Herr Hitler had made it very difficult for Shakespearean companies.

NORMAN. It'll be a chapter in the book, Sir. I hate to mention this but we're going to be short for the storm. We've no one to operate the wind machine, not if Mr Thornton is to play Fool. Mr. Thornton was ever so good on the wind machine. Madge knows the problem but she's very unsympathetic.

SIR. You tell Madge from me I must have the storm at full strength. What about Oxenby?

NORMAN. Not the most amenable of gentlemen.

SIR. Send him to me at the half. I'll have a word with him. And I'd better talk to Thornton, too.

NORMAN. You see? That's more like it. You're where you belong, doing what you know best, and you're yourself again. You start making up. I'll go and tell them to come and see you. I've cleaned the wig and beard. I'll see what we can do with these. Jumping on his hat indeed! Shan't be a minute. (NORMAN *goes.* SIR *looks at himself, then begins to black up.* NORMAN *returns*) Oh no, Sir! No! Not Othello!

(SIR *looks at him helplessly;* NORMAN *begins to clean his face with cold cream*)

SIR. The lines are fouled. Up on your short, down on your long. Do we have a dead for it? Instruct the puppeteer to renew the strings. The stuffing's escaping at the seams, straw from a scarecrow lies scattered down stage left.

(NORMAN *cleans* SIR's *face*)

NORMAN. I'd have given anything to see the play tonight. There's you all blacked up and Cordelia saying, "You begot me, bred me, loved me." Well, you see, ducky, this King Lear has been around a bit.

(SIR *laughs*)

SIR. We used to have a game when I was with Benson. We called it *Risqué*. You had to turn the line to get a *double entendre*. The best I ever heard was from a character man called Berriton. You know the line, "What fifty of my followers at a clap? Within a fortnight!"

NORMAN. Yes, I know the line, and the story.

SIR. One day, on the train call between Aberdeen and Liverpool, a journey I recommend as punishment for deserters, Berriton came out with "What, fifty of my followers with the clap? Within a fortnight!" (THEY BOTH *laugh*. NORMAN *has wiped* SIR's *face clean*. SIR *falls silent*. HE *looks at himself in the looking-glass*) Another blank page.

NORMAN. The time has come, if you don't mind my saying so, to stop waxing poetical and to wax a bit more practical.

(*Pause.* SIR *reaches out for a stick of make-up.*

Knock on the door)

NORMAN. Who?
IRENE. Irene. I've come for the triple crown.
SIR. Enter.

(IRENE, *dressed as a map-bearer in Lear, enters*)

SIR. (*Smiles*) Good evening, my child.
IRENE. Good evening, Sir.
SIR. All well?
IRENE. Thank you, Sir.
SIR. You've come for the triple crown.
IRENE. Yes, Sir.
SIR. Polish it well. I like it gleaming.
IRENE. Yes, Sir.
SIR. And return it to me well before curtain up. I like it on my head by the quarter.
IRENE. Yes, Sir.
SIR. And when I've used it on stage, see that it's returned to my room after the interval.
NORMAN. She has done it before, Sir.
SIR. I like to be certain. Here it is, my child.

(SHE *comes to him.* HE *pats her bottom*)

SIR. Pretty young thing, aren't you?
IRENE. Thank you, Sir. (SHE *goes.* SIR *stares fondly into space*)
NORMAN. Sir, it's time to age.

(SIR *looks at his make-up tray*)

SIR. (*In a panic*) They're all the same colour. Which stick do I use? I can't see the colours. (HE *looks at* NORMAN *helplessly.* NORMAN *goes to the basin and ewer, pours water, wets a bar of soap, and brings it to* SIR)

NORMAN. You start with the eyebrows.

SIR. Eyebrows?

NORMAN. Yes, Sir. You soap the eyebrows.

(SIR *applies soap to his eyebrows so that they are flattened*)

NORMAN. Good. Now Number Five. (HE *hands* SIR *the stick*) Just the mask you always say. Leave clean the upper lip and chin for the moustache and beard. And not too high on the forehead.

(SIR *applies the greasepaint*)

NORMAN. There. Easy as falling off a tightrope.

(SIR *continues to make up*)

SIR. In a Pythagorean future life I should certainly take up painting. My palette, a few brushes, a three-and-sixpenny canvas, a camp stool and no one to drive you.

NORMAN. No one drives you but yourself.

SIR. How dare you, how would you know, who says I drive myself? I'm driven, driven, driven—

NORMAN. I'm sorry, I didn't mean—

SIR. You have to believe in yourself and your destiny, you have to keep faith with your aspirations and allow yourself to be enslaved by them, and the bondage is everlasting. How dare you!

NORMAN. I'm sorry I mentioned it—

SIR. You have to learn to wait and wait and wait, and the moment comes when you launch your barque and take the rudder, then, oh my masters! beware. The effort to forget all you are risking, to face a first night audience before whom to lay open your soul, to put your entire life in jeopardy time after time, to bare your back to the stripes of the critics, to go on doing these things year after year, always with the terror increasing, because it's easier to climb than it is to hang on, and now d'you see why Benson wrote me after my first essay into management, "May you have the health and strength to go on"? On and on and on.

NORMAN. You should put that in the book.

SIR. Do they know what it means? Do they care? I hate the swines.

NORMAN. Who?

SIR. On and on and on—

NORMAN. All right, Sir, shall we go on and on and on with our make-up?

(*Pause.* SIR *looks helplessly at his make-up tray*)

SIR. There was a time when I had to paint in all the lines. Now I merely deepen what is already there. (HE *continues to make up.* MADGE *comes to the door, and knocks.* NORMAN *answers it*)

NORMAN. What now?

MADGE. How is he?

NORMAN. He'll be all right if he's left in peace.

MADGE. I want to see with my own eyes.

NORMAN. He is not to be disturbed.

MADGE. And what about the understudies?

NORMAN. He knows all about it, everything's in hand.

MADGE. The manager wants to know if he can let the house in.

NORMAN. Tell him yes.

MADGE. You realise now there's going to be an audience out there.

NORMAN. It'd be silly going through all this if there wasn't.

MADGE. Will he be ready on time? Will he be well enough?

NORMAN. Yes. (HE *closes the door on her*)

SIR. What is going on, who was that?

NORMAN. Just a minion, minioning.

SIR. Too many interruptions—my concentration—Norman!

NORMAN. Sir?

SIR. How does the play begin?

NORMAN. Which play, Sir?

SIR. Tonight's, tonight's, I can't remember my first line.

NORMAN. 'Attend the Lords of France and Burgundy, Gloucester.'

SIR. Yes, yes. What performance is this?

(NORMAN *consults a small notebook*)

NORMAN. Tonight will be your two hundred and twenty-seventh performance of the part, Sir.

SIR. Two hundred and twenty-seven Lears and I can't remember the first line.

NORMAN. We've forgotten something, if you don't mind my saying so.

(SIR *looks at him blankly*)

NORMAN. We have to sink our cheeks.

(SIR *applies the appropriate make-up*)

SIR. I shall look like this in my coffin.

NORMAN. And a broad straight line of Number Twenty down the nose. Gives strength, you say.

(SIR *adds to the line down the nose and studies the result.* NORMAN *pours a little Brown and Polson's cornflour into a bowl*)

SIR. Were you able to find any Brown and Polson's?

NORMAN. No, but I'm still looking. There's enough left for this tour. Now, we mix the white hard varnish with a little surgical spirit, don't we?

SIR. I know how to stick on a beard. I have been a depictor for over forty years and steered my own course for over thirty. You think I don't know how to affix a beard and moustache? You overstep the mark, boy. Don't get above yourself. (SIR *begins to apply the gum, and stick on the beard.* NORMAN *turns his back and has a nip of brandy*) I shall want a rest after the storm scene.

NORMAN. There's no need to tell me. I know.

SIR. Towel. (NORMAN *hands* SIR *a towel which* SIR *presses against the beard and moustache.* SIR *looks at himself in the looking-glass, and suddenly goes blank*) Something's missing. What's missing?

NORMAN. I don't want to get above myself, Sir, but how about the wig? (NORMAN *removes the wig from the block and hands it to* SIR) And shall we take extra care with the join tonight? On Tuesday Richard III looked as if he were wearing a peaked cap.

(SIR *puts on the wig and begins to colour the join.* HE *stops—*)

SIR. Hot, unbearably hot, going to faint—

(NORMAN *whips out the brandy bottle*)

NORMAN. Have a nip, it won't harm— (SIR *waves him away.* NORMAN *has a nip, puts the bottle away, and returns to* SIR, *who hasn't moved*) Oh, Sir, we mustn't give up, not now, not now. Let's highlight our lines.

(*Silence.* SIR *continues to add highlights*)

SIR. Imagine bombing the Grand Theatre, Plymouth. Barbarians. (*Pause*) I shall give them a good one tonight. (*Pause.* SIR *becomes alarmed*) Norman!

NORMAN. Sir?

SIR. What's the first line again? All this clitter-clatter-chitter-chatter—

NORMAN. 'Attend the Lords of France and Burgundy—'

SIR. You've put it from my head. You must keep silent when I'm dressing. I have to work to do, work, hard bloody labour, I have to carry the world tonight, the whole bloody universe—

NORMAN. Sir, Sir—

SIR. I can't remember the first line. A hundred thousand performances behind me and I have to ask you for the first line—

NORMAN. I'll take you through it—

SIR. Take me through it? Nobody takes you through it, you're *put* through it, night after night, and I haven't the strength.

NORMAN. Well, you're a fine one, I must say, you of all people, you disappoint me, if you don't mind my saying so. You, who always say self-pity is the most unattractive quality on stage or off. Who have you been working for all these years? The Ministry of Information? Struggle and survival, you say, that's all that matters, you say, struggle and survival. Well, we all bloody struggle, don't we? I struggle, I struggle, you think it's easy for me, well, I'll tell you something for nothing it isn't easy, not one little bit, neither the struggle nor the bloody survival. The whole world's struggling for bloody survival, so why can't you?

(*Silence*)

SIR. My dear Norman, I seem to have upset you.

I apologise. I understand. We cannot always be strong. There are dangers in covering the cracks.

NORMAN. Never mind about covering the cracks, what about the wig join?

(SIR *continues to make up*)

NORMAN. I'm sorry if I disturbed your concentration.

SIR. 'We both understand servitude, Alfonso.' What came next? What did I say to that?

NORMAN. 'Was it lack of ambition allowed me to endure what I have had to endure? It depends, your highness, what is meant by ambition. If ambition means a desire to sit in the seats of the mighty, yes, I have lacked such ambition. To me it has been a matter of some indifference where I have done my work. It has been the work itself which has been my chief joy.'

SIR. A fine memory, Norman.

NORMAN. My memory's like a policeman. Never there when you want it.

SIR. That was a play. And a money-maker. Greatly admired by clever charwomen and stupid clergymen. If I was twenty years younger I could still go on acting that kind of rubbish. But now I have to ascend the cosmos. And do they care? I hate the swines.

NORMAN. Shall we finish our eyebrows?

(SIR *combs the soaped eyebrows and whitens them.*
    IRENE *knocks on the door*)

IRENE. Half an hour, please, Sir. (SHE *goes*)

SIR. Already?

NORMAN. You were late in tonight, Sir.

SIR. Why hasn't she returned the triple crown? I like it on my head by now. Look!

NORMAN. What?

SIR. My hands. They're shaking.

NORMAN. Very effective in the part. Don't forget to make them up.

SIR. I can't keep them still. Do it for me.

(NORMAN *holds up his own hand, which is trembling*)

NORMAN. Look, it must be infectious. (NORMAN *makes up* SIR's *hands*)

SIR. I can face the division of my kingdom. I can cope with Fool. I can bear the reduction of my retinue. I can stomach the curses I have to utter. I can even face being whipped by the storm. But I dread the final entrance. To carry on Cordelia dead, to cry like the wind, howl, howl, howl. To lay her gently on the ground. To die. Have I the strength?

NORMAN. If you haven't the strength, no one has.

SIR. You're a good friend, Norman.

NORMAN. Thank you, Sir.

SIR. What would I do without you?

NORMAN. Manage on your own, I expect.

SIR. You'll be rewarded.

NORMAN. Pardon me while I get my violin.

SIR. Don't mock me. I may not have long.

NORMAN. My father used to say that. Lived to

be ninety-three. May still be alive for all I know. There! Albert Durer couldn't have done better. (HE *rises.* HE *powders* SIR's *hands.* HER LADYSHIP *enters, wigged and costumed as Cordelia but wearing a dressing-gown*)

HER LADYSHIP. Bonzo, how do you feel?

SIR. A little more myself, Pussy.

NORMAN. You see? Once he's assumed the disguise, he's a different man. Egad, Madam, thou hast a porcupine wit.

HER LADYSHIP. And you're sure you're able to go on?

SIR. On and on and on.

NORMAN. Don't start that again, please.

SIR. Pussy, I thought it was the Black One tonight.

HER LADYSHIP. My dear. Shall I fetch the cloak and tie it on as usual?

SIR. Yes. As usual.

HER LADYSHIP. Mr Thornton and Mr Oxenby are waiting outside to see you. Shall I ask them to come in?

SIR. I don't want to see Oxenby. He frightens me. Mind you, he's the best Iago I've ever had or seen and I include that four-foot-six ponce Sir Arthur Palgrove.

NORMAN. (*To* HER LADYSHIP) That's more like the Sir we know and love.

SIR. *Sir* Arthur Palgrove. He went on playing Hamlet till he was sixty-eight. There were more lines on his face than steps to the balcony. I saw his Lear. I was pleasantly disappointed. *Sir* Arthur Palgrove. Who advises His Majesty, answer me that?

(HE *continues to adjust his make-up putting the finishing touches.* HER LADYSHIP *draws* NORMAN *aside*)

HER LADYSHIP. You're a miracle-worker, Norman.

NORMAN. Thank you, your ladyship.

HER LADYSHIP. Here's a piece of chocolate for you.

NORMAN. Thank you, your ladyship.

HER LADYSHIP. It'll be all hands to the pump tonight, Norman.

NORMAN. A small part of the service, your ladyship.

HER LADYSHIP. Thank you. (SHE *goes*)

SIR. Don't suppose I didn't see that because I did. There are thousands of children in this beloved land of ours scavenging the larders for something sweet, and if only they came to me I could tell them of the one person in England who has an inexhaustible supply of chocolate. It is *I* who have to carry her on dead as Cordelia. It is *I* who have to lift her up, carry her in my arms. Thank Christ, I thought, for rationing, but no, she'd find sugar in a sand-dune.

NORMAN. Shall I show the actors in?

SIR. I don't—I don't want—

NORMAN. Sir, you have to see the actors. (HE *opens the door and calls*) Mr Thornton!

(GEOFFREY THORNTON, *an elderly actor, enters.* HE *wears a costume as Fool that is much too large for him*)

NORMAN. Mr Thornton to see you, Sir.

SIR. Well, Geoffrey . . . does the costume fit?

GEOFFREY. Mr Davenport-Scott was such a tall man.

SIR. Mr Davenport-Scott was a worm. You look— (HE *makes a vague gesture.* NORMAN *begins to help* SIR *into his Lear costume*) Do you know the lines?

GEOFFREY. Yes.

SIR. Don't keep me waiting for them.

GEOFFREY. Oh no.

SIR. Pace, pace, pace, pace, pace, pace.

GEOFFREY. Yes.

SIR. And keep out of my focus.

GEOFFREY. Yes.

SIR. The boom lights placed in the downstage wings are for me and me alone.

GEOFFREY. Yes, old man, I know.

SIR. You must find what light you can.

GEOFFREY. Right.

SIR. Let me hear you sing.

GEOFFREY. What?

SIR. 'He that has and a little tiny wit.'

GEOFFREY. (*Faltering*) 'He that has and—he that has—'

NORMAN. (*Singing*) 'He that has and a little tiny wit—'

GEOFFREY.

'He that has and a little tiny wit,

With hey, ho, the wind and the rain,

Must make content with his fortunes fit,

For the rain it raineth every day.'

SIR. All right, speak it, don't sing it. And in the storm scene, if you're going to put your arms round my legs as Davenport-Scott did, then round my calves not my thighs. He nearly ruptured me twice.

GEOFFREY. If you rather I didn't, old man—

SIR. Feel it, my boy, feel it, that's the only way. Whatever takes you.

GEOFFREY. Right.

SIR. But do not let too much take you. Remain within the bounds. And at all costs remain still when I speak.

GEOFFREY. Of course.

SIR. And no crying in the part.

GEOFFREY. Oh no.

SIR. *I* have the tears in this play.

GEOFFREY. I know.

SIR. Serve the playwright.

GEOFFREY. Yes.

SIR. And keep your teeth in.

GEOFFREY. It's only when I'm nervous—

SIR. You will be nervous, I guarantee it. There will be no extra payment for this performance. I believe your contract is 'play as cast'.

GEOFFREY. Yes.

SIR. Good fortune attend your endeavours.

GEOFFREY. Thank you, Sir.

(SIR *nods for him to leave.* NORMAN *sees him out*)

NORMAN. God bless, Geoffrey.

GEOFFREY. I'd rather face the Nazi hordes any time. (HE *goes*)

SIR. I hope Mr Churchill has better men in the Cabinet.

NORMAN. Mr Oxenby's waiting, Sir.

SIR. Oxenby? What—what—I can't—what does Oxenby want?

NORMAN. It's not what he wants, it's what we want, someone to operate the wind machine—

SIR. I don't want to see Oxenby, I can't bear the man, it's stifling in here—

NORMAN. We'll have no storm without him. (*Silence. NORMAN admits OXENBY, dressed as Edmund. HE limps. Pause*) Mr Oxenby to see you, Sir.

OXENBY. You wanted to see me.

SIR. I—I did I? I—Norman—why—?

NORMAN. Sir was wondering whether he could ask of you a favour.

OXENBY. He can ask.

NORMAN. You haven't been with us very long but I'm sure you've seen enough to know that we're not so much a company as one big happy family. We all muck in as required. As you will no doubt have heard, Mr Davenport-Scott will not be rejoining the company.

OXENBY. Yes, I've heard. You share a dressing-room with one or two of them, you hear nothing else. It upsets the pansy fraternity when one of their number is caught.

NORMAN. Because Mr Thornton is having to play Fool, and because our two elderly Knights are setting the hovel behind the front cloth during the storm, we have no one to operate the wind machine. We'd ask Mr Browne but he's really rather too fragile. We wondered if you would turn the handle.

OXENBY. In short, no. (*Silence*) Anything else? (*No response*) Has he read my play yet? (*No re-*

sponse. OXENBY *goes*)

SIR. Perhaps the Russians have had a setback on the Eastern front, Bolshevism will be the ruin of the theatre.

NORMAN. What are we going to do? Fancy not wanting to muck in.

SIR. He hates me. I feel his hatred. All I stand for he despises. I wouldn't read his play, not if he were Commissar of Culture.

NORMAN. I've read it.

SIR. Is there a part for me?

NORMAN. Yes, but you wouldn't credit the language.

SIR. He was ungenerous about Davenport-Scott. I hold no brief for buggers but where's the man's humanity? A fellow artist brought low and in the cells cannot be cause for rejoicing. I can see exactly what Oxenby's up to. He's writing plays for critics, not people.

NORMAN. Oughtn't we to be quiet for a bit, Sir?

SIR. Where's the girl with the triple crown?

NORMAN. Don't fuss.

(MADGE *knocks and enters with the triple crown*)

MADGE. Quarter of an hour, please, a few minutes late, here's the triple crown, I'm sorry, that girl, Irene—

SIR. The quarter, I can't, I'm not ready, tell them to go home, give them their money back, I can't, I hate the swines, I can't—I can't—

MADGE. What are you saying, do you want the performance cancelled?

NORMAN. No he doesn't—

SIR. How does it begin?

MADGE. For your own good—

SIR. How does it begin—?

MADGE. You'll never get through it—

NORMAN. He will, he will—

SIR. How does it begin?

NORMAN. Get out, he'll be good and ready when the curtain goes up—

MADGE. We've run out of time.

NORMAN. There's twenty minutes yet. We'll go up late, if necessary.

SIR. Leave me in peace! I can't remember the lines.

(MADGE *goes*)

SIR. Norman, Norman, how does it begin?

NORMAN. 'He hath been out nine years and away he shall again.' (*Imitates a trumpet fanfare*) 'The King is coming.' (*Silence*) 'Attend the Lords of France and Burgundy, Gloucester.'

SIR. 'Attend the Lords of France and Burgundy, Gloucester.'

NORMAN. 'I shall, my liege.'

(*Pause*)

SIR. Yes?

NORMAN. 'Meantime we shall express our darker—'

SIR. 'Meantime we shall express our darker purpose.'

(*Pause*)

NORMAN. 'Give me the map—'

SIR. Don't tell me, don't tell me, I know it, I'll ask for it if I need it, I have played the part before, you know. 'Meantime we shall express our darker purpose.' (*Long pause*) Yes?

NORMAN. 'Give me the map there.'

SIR. 'Give me the map there.' Don't tell me, don't tell me. (*Long silence*) 'What do I fear?'

NORMAN. Wrong. 'Know that we have divided—'

SIR. (*Continuing*) 'Myself? there's none else by. True, I talk of dreams, which are the children of an idle brain.'

NORMAN. Wrong play, wrong play—

SIR. 'I will move storms, I will condole in some measure—'

NORMAN. That's another wrong play—

SIR. 'I pray you all, tell me what they deserve that do conspire my death with devilish plots of damned witchcraft, and that have prevail'd upon my body with their hellish charms? Can this cockpit hold the vasty fields of France? Men should be what they seem. My name's Macbeth! I have lived long enough!'

NORMAN. Now look what you've gone and done—

SIR. What—?

NORMAN. Go out, go out, you've quoted the Scots tragedy—

SIR. Did I? Macb—? Did I? Oh Christ—

NORMAN. Out—(SIR *goes*) Turn round three times. Knock. (SIR *turns and knocks*) Come in. (SIR *re-enters*) Swear.

SIR. Pisspots. (SIR *holds his head and stands swaying slightly.* NORMAN *looks at him despairingly.* HER LADYSHIP *enters carrying a cloak and dressed as Cordelia.* SIR *looks at her and takes her face in his hands* 'And my poor fool is hang'd. No, no, no life! Why should a dog, a horse, a rat have life And thou no breath at all? Thou'lt come no more. Never, never, never, never, never!'

(*Silence*)

NORMAN. Welcome back, Sir, you'll be all right.

(SIR *puts on the triple crown.* HER LADYSHIP *puts the cloak around* SIR's *shoulders. A ritual*)

HER LADYSHIP. (*Kissing his hand*) Struggle, Bonzo.
SIR. (*Kissing her hand*) Survival, Pussy.

(*Knock on door*)

IRENE. (*Off*) Five minutes, please, Sir.
NORMAN. Thank you.
SIR. Let us descend and survey the scene of battle. (THEY *are about to go when the air-raid sirens sound.* THEY *freeze*) The night I played my first Lear there was a real thunderstorm. Now they send bombs. How much more have I to endure? We are to speak Will Shakespeare tonight and they will go to any lengths to prevent me.
NORMAN. I shouldn't take it so personally, Sir—
SIR. (*Looking heavenward*) Bomb, bomb, bomb us into oblivion if you dare, but each word I speak

will be a shield against your savagery, each line I utter protection from your terror.

NORMAN. I don't think they can hear you, Sir.

SIR. Swines! Barbarians! (SIR *begins to shiver uncontrollably, and to whimper*)

NORMAN. Oh Sir, just as we were winning.

HER LADYSHIP. Perhaps it's timely. He can't go on. Look at him. (SHE *comforts him. To* NORMAN) Fetch Madge.

SIR. Norman!

NORMAN. Sir.

SIR. Get me down to the stage. By Christ, no squadron of Fascist Bolsheviks will stop me now. (HE *continues to shiver.* HER LADYSHIP *and* NORMAN *look at each other uncertainly*) Do as I say!

(NORMAN *and* HER LADYSHIP *help him*)

HER LADYSHIP. Who'll make the announcement?

SIR. Davenport-Scott, of course.

(*Silence*)

NORMAN. Oh dear. Mr. Davenport-Scott isn't here tonight. Everyone else is in costume.

SIR. You then, Norman.

NORMAN. Me, Sir? No, Sir. I can't appear!

SIR. You, Norman.

NORMAN. But, Sir. I shall never remember what to say—

SIR. Do not argue. I have given my orders, I have enough to contend with—

NORMAN. But, Sir, Sir, I'm not equipped.

SIR. Do it. (HER LADYSHIP *helps him. As* THEY
go—) Why can't I stop shaking?

(Sirens continue loudly. Bombs begin to fall. NORMAN
*swigs deeply from the brandy bottle and finishes
it. Sirens. Bomb. Blackout. Sirens and bombs
continue. A bright spotlight on* NORMAN)

NORMAN. (*Softly*) Ladies and gentlemen ... (*Louder*) Ladies and gentlemen, the—the warning has
just gone. An air-raid is in progress. We shall proceed
with the performance. Will those—will those who
wish to live—will those who wish to leave do so
as quietly as possible? Thank you. (HE *stands rooted
to the spot. Bombs*)

BLACKOUT

END OF ACT I

ACT II

The wings. Darkness. The air-raid continues. NOR-MAN's *voice is heard.*

NORMAN. (*Softly*) Ladies and gentlemen ... (*Louder*) Ladies and gentlemen, the—the warning has just gone. An air-raid is in progress. We shall proceed with the performance. Will those—will those who wish to live—will those who wish to leave do so as quietly as possible? Thank you.

(*Sound of string quartet playing finale of selections from 'The Mikado'. Light on* MADGE *in prompt corner. Music ends. Applause*)

MADGE. Stand by. Stand by on tabs. House lights to a half. (SHE *peers through peep-hole at the auditorium. Expectant murmurs from audience*) Cue timpani. (*Timpani starts a steady beat*) House lights out. (*Pause*) Cueing grams. (*A recorded fanfare sounds*) Cue drum role. (*Timpani breaks into a roll.* MADGE *cues tabs*) Stand by on stage. Go Elex. Curtain going up.

(*Light grows to reveal* NORMAN, *who is carrying a whip, a towel and a tray on which stands a glass of stout and a powder puff.* HE *is just*

50

entering the wings. The following continues on-
stage at the same time as the play begins off-
stage. Offstage we hear the voices of GLOUCESTER,
KENT *and* OXENBY [*as* EDMUND] *as* THEY *begin*
the play)

KENT. I thought the King had more affected the
Duke of Albany than Cornwall.

GLOUCESTER. It did always seem so to us . . .

NORMAN. Geoffrey, was I all right? The announcement. Was I effective?

KENT. Is not this your son, my Lord?

GLOUCESTER. His breeding, sir, hath been at my
charge: I have so often blushed to acknowledge
him, that now I am brazed to it.

NORMAN. (*Contd*) Your ladyship, was I all right?

KENT. I cannot conceive you.

HER LADYSHIP. Better than Mr Davenport-Scott.

GLOUCESTER. Sir, this young fellow's mother could;
whereupon she grew round-wombed . . .

NORMAN. Really? Do you mean it? I was ever
so nervous. Do you think anyone noticed the fluff?
"Will those who wish to live." Could have kicked
myself. Was I really all right?

HER LADYSHIP. You were fine.

NORMAN. Did he say anything?

HER LADYSHIP. No.

GLOUCESTER. (*Contd*) But I have a son, sir, by
order of law, some year elder than this who yet
is no dearer in my account . . . Do you know this
noble gentleman, Edmund?

EDMUND. No, my Lord.

GLOUCESTER. My Lord of Kent; remember him here-
after as my honourable friend.

EDMUND. My services to your lordship.

KENT. I must love you, and sue to know you better.

EDMUND. Sir, I shall study deserving.

GLOUCESTER. He hath been out nine years, and
away he shall again . . .

MADGE. Cueing grams.

(*Fanfare*)

GLOUCESTER. (*Contd*) The King is coming.

MADGE. (*Contd*) Stand by please, your ladyship,
stand by please, Sir.

(*Fanfare. Trumpet sounds from prompt speaker.* HER
LADYSHIP *goes on. Scattered applause*)

MADGE. (*Contd*) Cueing timpani, Sir. (MADGE *flicks
a switch. The green cue light goes on.* IRENE *begins
to beat the timpani in a slow rhythm.* MADGE *flicks
the switch repeatedly, which makes the green light
flash.* IRENE *increases the rhythm of the timpani*)
Stand by, Sir. Cueing the King's fanfare.

(*A great fanfare sounds.* NORMAN *tries to help*
SIR *rise.* SIR *remains seated and continues to
shiver*)

NORMAN. Sir, it's your cue.

(SIR *does not move.* IRENE *continues to drum*)

NORMAN. (*Contd*) Her Ladyship's entered. Quite a nice round, too. Now it's your turn. Come along, Sir.

(*The fanfare ends.* SIR *still does not move.* MADGE *switches off cue light and* IRENE *stops drumming.* MADGE *goes to* SIR *and* NORMAN)

MADGE. You see? What did I say?
GLOUCESTER. The King is coming.
NORMAN. Please, Sir, I implore you.

(*Silence*)

NORMAN. (*Contd*) Sir, you're on. You're on.
OXENBY. Methought I saw the King.

(BOTH MADGE *and* NORMAN *try to get him on*)

KENT. Methought so, too.
NORMAN. (*Contd*) Please, Sir, it's your entrance. Mr Oxenby's having to extemporise.
OXENBY. Methought I saw him, his procession formed, a hundred knights his escort, sombre they looked, their muted colours of a tone with the bleak heathland which is our kingdom.

(THEY *try to get* SIR *to his feet.* HE *shivers uncontrollably*)

HER LADYSHIP. The King, my father, was, methought, behind me. From our camp we marched, a goodly distance. I ahead, as is our custom. Perchance he rested, for age has not the spring of youth.

(*Murmurs from the audience*)

NORMAN. (*Contd*) Sir, the natives are getting restless. (*To* MADGE) Sound the fanfare again.
(MADGE *goes to* IRENE *and whispers instructions.* NORMAN *hoists* SIR *to his feet*)

OXENBY. Ah! Methinks I see the King.

(SIR *sits again*)

OXENBY. (*Contd*) No, I was mistook.

(*A bomb explodes quite close.* NORMAN *gets* SIR *to his feet again and guides him towards the stage*)

OXENBY. (*Contd*) My Lord, with thy consent I shall to his majestic side, there to discover his royal progress.

(OXENBY *comes into the wings from the stage*)

OXENBY. Is he coming or isn't he?
NORMAN. Yes!

(OXENBY *goes back*)

OXENBY. I am assured, my Lord, the King is coming.

MADGE. Cue the King's fanfare again.

(*The fanfare sounds. Another bomb explodes quite close*)

NORMAN. Struggle and survival, Sir, it's a full house. (SIR *comes to himself*) 'Attend the Lords of France and Burgundy, Gloucester.' (*To* MADGE) Cue the Knights, cue the Knights.

MADGE. (*To the* KNIGHTS) Go on, Go on. (SHE *switches off the cue light.* IRENE *stops beating, runs to collect the map and stands by for her entrance*)

NORMAN. (*To* IRENE) Enter, for God's sake.

(NORMAN *takes out a fresh quarter bottle of brandy and drinks deeply. Blackout. Bombs and antiairchraft guns continue. Dim light.* NORMAN, MADGE, GEOFFREY *and* OTHERS *watch the stage and hear* SIR's *voice*)

SIR.

No, you unnatural hags,

I will have such revenges on you both

That all the world shall—I will do such things—

What they are yet I know not—but they shall be

The terrors of the earth.

You think I'll weep;
No, I'll not weep; I have full cause of weeping,
    but this heart
Shall break into a hundred thousand flaws
Or ere I'll weep. O fool! I shall go mad.

(*The green light glows and* NORMAN *cracks the
    thunder sheet. The air-raid continues as* SIR *re-
    turns to the wings. Lights*)

KENT.
    For confirmation that I am much more
    Than my out-wall, open this purse, and take
    What it contains. If you shall see Cordelia—
MADGE. Stand by the storm.
KENT. (*Contd*)
    As doubt not but you shall—show her this ring,
    And she will tell you who your fellow is
    That yet you do not know.
        Fie on this storm!
    I will go seek the King.

(*The 'All Clear' sounds*)

GENTLEMAN. Give me your hand. Have you no
more to say?
SIR. (*Looking heavenwards*) Swines! Just when
you need them they run away.
KENT.
    Few words, but, to effect, more than all yet;
    That, when we have found the King—in which
        your pain

That way, I'll this—he that first lights on him
Holla the other.

MADGE. Go storm.

(SHE *switches a switch. The red cue light glows.
Green warning light. The thunder begins,* NOR-
MAN *and* IRENE *managing between them.* SIR
and GEOFFREY *go on.* HER LADYSHIP *watches
the stage.* OXENBY *stands apart, also watching.*
HER LADYSHIP *runs to the thunder crew*)

SIR. Blow, winds, and crack your cheeks ...! (HIS
voice is drowned by the noise of the storm)

HER LADYSHIP. Louder! Louder! (SHE *returns to
watch the stage as the thunder increases.* HER LADY-
SHIP *returns to the crew*) Louder, louder, he wants
it louder!

(*The noise increases.* NORMAN *works frantically.*
HER LADYSHIP *comes to them again*)

HER LADYSHIP. (*Contd*) Louder! Louder!

(NORMAN *and* IRENE *give all* THEY *have.* OXENBY,
*who has been watching them, takes over the
thunder sheet.* HER LADYSHIP *takes charge of
the wind machine. The sound of a mighty tempest
is reproduced. And when the sound is overpower-
ing and at its loudest*: *blackout.* SIR *comes raging
into the wings. Lights on* SIR *and* NORMAN)

SIR. (*Mad with rage*) *Where was the storm?* I ask for cataracts and hurricanes and I am given trickles and whistles. I demand oak-cleaving thunderbolts and you answer with farting flies. I *am* the storm! I am the wind and the spit and the fire and the pother and I am fed with nothing but muffled funeral drums. Christ Almighty, God forgive them for they know not what they do. I am driven deaf by whispers. Norman, Norman, you have thwarted me. (SIR *marches to his dressing room followed by* NORMAN) I was there, within sight, I had only to be spurred upwards and the glory was mine for the plucking and there was nought, zero, silence, a breeze, a shower, a collision of cotton-wool, the flapping of butterfly wings. I want a tempest not a drizzle. Something will have to be done. I demand to know what happened tonight to the storm! (SIR *sinks down on to his couch*)

NORMAN. I'm pleased you're pleased. I've never known you not complain when you've really been at it, and tonight, one could say without fear of contradiction, you were at it. Rest now. (SIR *lies back.* NORMAN *covers him with a rug, mops his brow and makes him comfortable. Then* HE *turns gas ring up so that kettle boils, makes* SIR *tea and feeds it to him*) You've got the whole interval. Try to sleep. You've been through it, or been put through it, which ever you prefer and you need quiet, as the deaf mute said to the piano tuner. Mighty, Her Ladyship thought you were tonight, she did, that was the word she used, mighty. Of course, I cannot comment on the storm scene but I did hear, 'O Reason not the need'. Tremble-making. Never seen you so full of the real thing, if you don't mind my saying so, Sir. And wasn't Geoffrey agile as Fool? For a man of his age. Kept well-down-stage, never once got in your light, much less obtrusive than Mr Davenport-Scott. In every way. And here's something funny. In the storm scene, when we were beating ourselves delirious, and I was having to jump between thunder-sheet and timpani like a juggler with rubber balls and Indian clubs, Mr Oxenby came to our aid uninvited. Cracked and clapped he did with abandon. Not a word said, just gave assistance when assistance was needed. Afterwards, just before the interval, I thanked him. "Get stuffed," he said which wasn't nice, and added scornfully, "I don't know why I helped." And I said, "Because we're a band of brothers, and you're one of us in spite of yourself." I did, that's what I said, quite unabashed. He hobbled away, head down, and if he was given to muttering, he'd have muttered. Darkly. (*Pause*) More tea? Are you asleep, Sir?

SIR. To be driven thus. I hate the swines.

NORMAN. Who? Who is it you hate? The critics?

SIR. The critics? Hate the critics? I have nothing but compassion for them. How can one hate the crippled, the mentally deficient and the dead? Bastards.

NORMAN. Who then?

SIR. Who then what?

NORMAN. Who then what is it you hate?

SIR. Let me rest, Norman, you must stop questioning me, let me rest. But don't leave me till I'm asleep. Don't leave me alone. (*Pause*) I am a spent force. (*Pause*) My days are numbered.

(*Silence.* NORMAN *watches him, then takes out his brandy bottle but finds it empty.* HE *tip-toes out of the room. In the corridor* HE *meets* HER LADYSHIP, *carrying a sewing-bag*)

HER LADYSHIP. Is he asleep?

NORMAN. I think so.

HER LADYSHIP. I'll sit with him.

NORMAN. Don't wake him, will you, your ladyship. He's ever so tired. (HE *goes.* HER LADYSHIP *enters* SIR's *dressing room and deliberately makes a noise.* SIR *starts*)

SIR. Is it my cue?

HER LADYSHIP. No. It's still the interval. (SHE *sits and begins to darn pairs of tights*) I have things to say.

SIR. Norman tells me you thought I was mighty tonight.

HER LADYSHIP. I never said anything of the kind. He makes these things up.

(*Pause*)

SIR. What have you to say?

HER LADYSHIP. What I always have to say.

SIR. You know my answer.

HER LADYSHIP. You've worked hard. You've saved. Enough's enough. Tonight, in your curtain speech, make the announcement.

SIR. I can't.

HER LADYSHIP. You won't.

SIR. I've no choice.

HER LADYSHIP. You'll die. Or end up a vegetable. Well, that's your affair. But you're not going to drag me with you.

SIR. I am helpless, Pussy. I do what I'm told. I cower, frightened of being whipped. I am driven.

HER LADYSHIP. Driven, no. Obstinate, yes, cruel, yes, ruthless, yes.

SIR. Don't.

HER LADYSHIP. You know where your priorities lie. Whatever you do is to your advantage and to no one else's. Talk about being driven. You make yourself sound like a disinterested stage-hand. You do nothing without self-interest. Self. You. Alone.

SIR. Pussy, please, I'm sinking, don't push me further into the mud—

HER LADYSHIP. Sir. Her Ladyship. Fantasies. For God's sake, you're a third-rate actor-manager on a tatty tour of the provinces, not some Colossus bestriding the narrow world. Sir. Her Ladyship. Look at me. Darning tights. Look at you. Lear's hovel is luxury compared to this.

SIR. I'm not well, I have half of Lear's lifetime yet to live, I have to lift you in my arms, I have howl, howl, howl yet to speak.

HER LADYSHIP. Sir. Her Ladyship. We're a laughing-stock. You'd never get a knighthood because the King doesn't possess a double-edged sword. The only honour you'll ever get is when you go on stage and we all bow.

(*Silence*)

SIR. I thought tonight I caught sight of him. Or saw myself as he sees me. Speaking 'Reason not the need,' I was suddenly detached from myself. My thoughts flew. And I was observing from a great height. Go on, you bastard, I seemed to be saying

or hearing. Go on, you've more to give, don't hold
back more, more, more. And I was watching Lear.
Each word he spoke was fresh invented. I had no
knowledge of what came next, what fate awaited
him. The agony was in the moment of acting created.
I saw an old man and the old man was me. And
I knew there was more to come. But what? Bliss,
partial recovery, more pain and death. All this I
knew I had yet to see. Outside myself, do you
understand? Outside myself. (HE *holds out his hand.*
SHE *does not take it*) Don't leave me. I'll rest
easy if you stay. Don't ask of me the impossible.
Otherwise, I know, without you, in darkness, I'll
see a locked door, a sign turned in the window,
closed, gone away, and a drawn blind.

HER LADYSHIP. I'll stay till Norman returns.

SIR. Longer. I meant longer. Please. Please, Pussy. Reassure me. I'm sick—

HER LADYSHIP. I should have left you in Baltimore
on the last American tour. I should have accepted
Mr Feldman's offer and taken the 20th Century west.

(*Pause*)

SIR. Feldman didn't think I'd photograph well.
Swine. I hate the cinema. I believe in living things.

HER LADYSHIP. How quickly one's looks go.

SIR. They haven't built a camera large enough
to record me.

HER LADYSHIP. I wouldn't have minded a modest
success.

SIR. Why they knighted that dwarf Arthur Palgrove I shall never know. "Rise, Sir Arthur," said

the King, "But, Sir, I wasn't kneeling." Not once
in his whole career did he put a toe outside London.

HER LADYSHIP. I liked America.

SIR. I shall never forgive them for what they wrote
about me.

(*Knock on the door*)

IRENE. (*Off*) Act Two beginners, please, Sir.

SIR. I must rest now, Pussy. I want peace.

HER LADYSHIP. All you want is to have your cake
and to eat it.

SIR. I've never seen any point in having cake
unless one's going to eat it. (HE *laughs.* NORMAN
re-enters)

NORMAN. Everything jolly?

SIR. Don't you know what knocking is?

NORMAN. Please, Sir, not in front of Her Ladyship.
I've been mingling. You should hear what they think
out there. I've never known an interval like it. Michelangelo, William Blake, God knows who else you
reminded them of.

SIR. Michelangelo, did they?

NORMAN. And Blake.

HER LADYSHIP. I'm going to my room.

SIR. Please stay.

HER LADYSHIP. You must rest, Bonzo, mustn't he,
Norman?

NORMAN. Yes, he must.

SIR. Pussy—

(SHE *goes*)

SIR. Be gentle with Her Ladyship.

NORMAN. I'm always gentle with Her Ladyship.
SIR. Especially gentle.
NORMAN. Why?
SIR. Time of life.
NORMAN. You mean hot flushes and dizzy spells.
SIR. She's become very preoccupied with herself.
NORMAN. Sounds like a bad attack of change.
SIR. Be gentle. I don't want her hurt.
NORMAN. Sleep now. Is there anything else you want?
SIR. Only oblivion.
NORMAN. That'll come sooner or later and I hope later. I'll wake you in plenty of time so you can enter fantastically dressed in wild flowers. Sleep tight, don't let the fleas bite. (HE *goes.* SIR *suddenly starts, rises, finds his exercise book and, straining to see, begins to write.* IRENE *knocks gently on the door*)
SIR. Who?
IRENE. Irene. I'm returning the triple crown, Sir.
SIR. Come.

(SHE *enters the room*)

SIR. Put it down.

(SHE *does so.* HE *continues to write. Pause*)

IRENE. Sir, will it disturb you if I say something?
SIR. It depends on what it is.
IRENE. I just wanted to thank you.
SIR. For what?
IRENE. The performance this evening.

SIR. It's not over yet.

IRENE. I felt honoured to be on the stage.

(*Pause*)

SIR. Open that drawer you will find a photograph of me.

(SHE *does so.* HE *inscribes it*)

IRENE. I love coming into this room. I can feel the power. And the mystery. In days gone by this would have been the place where the High Priests robed. I felt frightened. As though I'm trespassing.

SIR. A kindred spirit. (THEY *look at each other*) Lock that door. (SHE *does so*) Come nearer—

IRENE. Irene.

SIR. Irene. And you want to act.

IRENE. Yes.

SIR. Passionately?

IRENE. Yes.

SIR. With every fibre of your being?

IRENE. Yes.

SIR. To the exclusion of all else?

IRENE. Yes.

SIR. You must be prepared to sacrifice what most people call life.

IRENE. I am.

(*Long pause*)

SIR. Your birth sign?

IRENE. Scorpio.

(*In the corridor* NORMAN *enters, comes to the door,
    tries it gently but finds it locked.* HE *listens
    at the key-hole*)

SIR. Good. Ambition, secretiveness, loyalty and cap-
able of great jealousy. Essential qualities for the
theatre. Have you good legs? (SHE *shrugs*) Come
closer. Let me see. (SHE *raises her skirt*) Higher.
(SHE *does so*) Too good. All the best actresses have
legs like tree-trunks. (HE *feels her thighs*) There's
not much to you. (HE *feels her hips*) Such small
bones. (HIS *hands wander up to her breasts*) Are
you getting enough to eat? (HE *takes her face in
his hands and seems about to kiss her*) So young,
so young. (*Suddenly, in one movement* HE *lifts her
bodily into his arms.* SHE *cries out. A great roar*)
That's more like it! (HE *staggers, lowers her to
the ground, then waves her away*) Too late, too
late.

(SHE *runs to the door, unlocks it, goes into the
    corridor and comes face to face with* NORMAN,
    door. SIR *sits, scribbles, then rests*)

NORMAN. Well now, my dainty duck, my dear-o.
IRENE. Let go of me.
NORMAN. What was all that about?

(*Pause*)

IRENE. He seems better.
NORMAN. Better than what or whom as the case
may be?

IRENE. I didn't think he'd get through the performance tonight.

NORMAN. He's not through it yet. (*Pause*) I'm waiting.

IRENE. For what?

NORMAN. A graphic description of events. Out with it. Or I shall slap your face. Hard. You had better know that my parentage is questionable, and that I can be vicious when roused.

IRENE. I thought we were friends.

NORMAN. I thought so, too, Irene. I shall long remember welcoming you into the company in the prop room of the Palace Theatre, Newark-on-Trent, the smell of size and carpenter's glue, the creaking of skips and you locked in the arms of the Prince of Morocco, a married man, ever such a comic sight with his tights round his ankles and you smeared black. I said "Don't worry, mum's the word, but don't let it happen again." We talked, brewed tea on a paint-stained gas-ring. You expressed gratitude and I said, "Now you're one of the family." And this is how you repay me.

IRENE. What am I supposed to have done?

NORMAN. You tell me.

IRENE. About what?

NORMAN. About Sir. The Guv'nor, the Chief, Father, Him from whom all favours flow. You know who Sir is, Irene.

IRENE. I'm late. I have to help Her Ladyship with her armour

NORMAN. Her Ladyship's armour will keep. Perhaps you didn't hear my question. What did Sir do?

IRENE. I'm not telling you—

(HE *grabs her closer and threatens to strike her*)

NORMAN. I'll mark you for life, ducky.

IRENE. You strike me and I'll tell him, I'll tell Sir, I'll tell Sir, I will, I'll tell Sir—

(HE *lets go of her*)

NORMAN. Tell Sir? On me? I quake in my boots. I shan't be able to eat my tea. Tell Sir? Gadzooks, madam, the thought of it, you telling Sir on me. Ducky, in his present state, which totters between confusion and chaos, to tell Sir anything at all would take a louder voice and clearer diction than that possessed by the most junior member of this Shakespearean troupe, the assistant stage-manager, dog's body, general understudy, map-carrier and company mattress, namely you. You won't be able to tell Sir you'd let him touch your tits on a Thursday matinee in Aberystwyth. Tell Sir. You think I don't know the game? You think I've dressed the rotten bugger for sixteen bloody years, nursed him, spoiled him, washed his sweat-sodden doublet and hose and his foul underpants night after night without knowing every twist and turn of what is laughingly known as his mind? Never mind tell Sir. I'll tell you. He did something, something unseen and furtive, something that gave him pleasure. "That's more like it!" More like what, Irene? I have to know all that occurs. I have to know all he does.

(*Pause*)

IRENE. He lifted me up in his arms.

NORMAN. Lifted you up?

IRENE. And I understood, I understood what he meant. "So young, so young," he said, and lifted me up. "That's more like it," he cried and I knew, cradled in his arms, that it was youth and newness he was after—(NORMAN *laughs*)—why do you laugh? I was there, it happened, it's true, I felt it. He was trembling and so was I. Up in his arms, part of him, "that's more like it," and he lowered me, waved me away and I ran off. Youth. And with my eyes closed I imagined what it would be like to be carried on by him, Cordelia, dead in his arms, Young.

NORMAN. Never mind a young Cordelia, ducky, he wants a light Cordelia. Light, ducky, light. Look at yourself. Look at Her Ladyship.

IRENE. You don't understand. He needs youth—

NORMAN. "That's more like it." You're lighter than she is, ducky. (HE *laughs. Pause*) You're not the first to be placed on the scales. How do you think Her Ladyship got the job? Her Ladyship, when a slip of a girl, went from map-carrier to youngest daughter overnight. I remember it well. That was the tour the Doge of Venice gave Launcelot Gobbo clap.

(IRENE *begins to cry softly*)

NORMAN. It's not youth or talent or star quality

he's after, ducky, but a moderate eater. (*Pause*)
We could cope with anything in those days. Turmoil
was his middle name. (NORMAN *sways a little,
then controls himself.* HE *becomes tearful but holds
back*) So. Ducky. Keep well away. The old days
are gone, the days of vim and vigour, what's to
come is still unsure. Trip no further, pretty sweeting.
We can't have any distractions. Not anymore. Not
if things are to be lovely. And painless. (*Pause*)
Don't disobey me, will you? The fateful words, "You
finish on Saturday" have a decidedly sinister ring—

(HER LADYSHIP *appears*)
—two rings, and bangles right up to the elbow.

HER LADYSHIP. There you are. You're late with
my armour. (SHE *goes*)

NORMAN. Off you go, ducky You have to find
another canoe to paddle. Ours, I'm afraid, has holes.
(IRENE *goes.* NORMAN *swigs from his brandy bottle.*
HE *goes into* SIR's *dressing room. Gently,* HE *shakes*
SIR *awake*) Fantastically dressed in wild flowers.

(SIR *rises. In silence* NORMAN *helps him to change
costumes and then bedecks him in wild flowers*)

SIR. Michelangelo, did they?
NORMAN. And Blake.
SIR. I knew what they mean. Moral grandeur.

(*Pause*)

NORMAN. I talked to the girl. She's not as light

as she looks. We're none of us strong enough for a change of cast.

(*Pause.* SIR, *suddenly and fiercely, embraces*)

SIR. You cannot be properly paid. *In pectora,* I name you friend. The debt is all mine. And I shall find a way to repay you. I must, must settle all my debts.

NORMAN. Don't, you're making me tearful—

SIR. (*Letting go of him*) God, your breath smells of stale tights. How much have you had?

NORMAN. Not enough.

SIR. Iago, Iago—

NORMAN. Wrong play.

SIR. I have to wake in bliss, I have to carry on Her Ladyship, I need you sober.

NORMAN. I am. Sober. Diction perfect. Deportment steady. Temper serene. (NORMAN *smiles*)

SIR. It is no laughing matter! (*Pause*) The final push. I hope you're up to it.

NORMAN. (*Under his breath*) And you, dear.

SIR. What?

NORMAN. And you, Lear.

(THEY *begin to go. Lights fade to blackout. Drums. Trumpets. Clash of swords Light grows. The wings.* SIR, HER LADYSHIP *and* NORMAN *stand in readiness,* IRENE *by the timpani*)

KENT.
    I am come
    To bid my King and master aye good-night;

Is he not here?

ALBANY. Speak, Edmund, where's the King?. .

(SIR *spits on his hands*)

HER LADYSHIP. I wish you wouldn't do that. You remind me of a labourer.

EDMUND.

    I pant for life; some good I mean to do
    Despite of mine own nature.
      Quickly send,
    Be brief in it, to the castle; for my writ
    Is on the life of Lear and on Cordelia.
    Nay, send in time.

(SIR *lifts* HER LADYSHIP *in his arms and carries her on. Those in the wings watch*)

ALBANY.

    Run, run! O run!...
    Haste thee, for thy life.

SIR.

    Howl, howl, howl, howl! O!
      you are men of stones:
    Had I your tongues and eyes, I'd use them so
    That heaven's vaults should crack She's gone
      for ever.
    I know when one is dead, and when one lives;
    She's dead as earth . . .

(*Lights fade to blackout. Lights up again quickly*)

KENT. Break, heart; I prithee, break.

ALBANY.

The weight of this sad time we must obey;
Speak what we feel, not what we ought to say.
The oldest hath borne most: we that are young,
Shall never see so much, nor live so long.

(IRENE *drums a slow, sombre rhythm*)

MADGE. Cue curtain down.

(*Sound of curtain falling. Applause.* SIR *comes into the wings*)

SIR (*Looking heavenwards*) We've done it, Will, we've done it.

MADGE. Stand by for curtain-calls. Curtain going up.

(*The* COMPANY *take their curtain calls*)

MADGE. Stand by for your curtain-call, Sir.

(SIR *goes on for his call. Thunderous applause and cheers. Lights change to a solitary light, bright and harsh.* SIR *steps into the light and* NORMAN *stands just behind him in shadow. Applause and cheers continue until* SIR *raises his hand for silence*)

SIR. My lords, ladies and gentlemen. Thank you for the manner in which you have received the greatest tragedy in our language. We live in danger-ous times. Our civilization is under threat from the forces of darkness, and we, humble actors, do all in our power to fight as soldiers on the side of right in the great battle. Our most cherished ambition is to keep the best alive of our drama, to serve the greatest poet-dramatist who has ever lived, and we are animated by nothing else than to educate the nation in his works by taking his plays to every corner of our beloved island. Tomorrow night we shall give—

NORMAN. *Richard III.*

SIR. —*King Richard III.* I myself will play the hunchback king. On Saturday afternoon my lady-wife will play—

NORMAN. Portia.

SIR. —Portia, and I the badly-wronged Jew in *The Merchant of Venice*, a play you may think of greater topicality than ever. On Saturday night—

NORMAN. *Lear.*

SIR. —On Saturday night we shall essay once more the tragedy you have this evening witnessed and I myself shall again undergo the severest test known to an actor. Next week, God willing, we shall be in—

NORMAN. Eastbourne.

SIR. —Eastbourne. I trust your friends and relatives there will, on your recommendation, discover source for refreshment, as you seem to have done by your warm indication, in the glorious words we are privileged to speak. For the generous manner in which you have received our earnest endeavours, on behalf of my lady wife, my company and myself, I remain your humble and obedient servant, and can no other answer make but thanks and thanks, and ever thanks. (*Bows. Applause.* HE *steps out of the light. Applause continues. Light fades. Light on* SIR *as* HE *steps back from the curtain call and collapses in* NORMAN'S *arms. While* NORMAN *helps* SIR *to his dressing room*—) I'm getting weaker. Today I'm weaker than I was yesterday. Tomorrow I shall be weaker still. I gather my strength but I need more and more strength. And it isn't there. I'm weaker, weakened, weakning. I'm at end.

NORMAN. Until tomorrow.

SIR. Tomorrow I'll have to gather myself again. My mind is not my own. I remember so little of what happens. Each day the sea is rougher. The ropes blister my hands. I worry about you. What will you do?

NORMAN. As best I can.

(THEY *have reached the dressing room and* SIR *has begun removing his wig and beard*)

SIR. What is the play tomorrow?

NORMAN. Richard III.

SIR. Again? Who planned this tour?

NORMAN. You did.

SIR. Slavery, bloody slavery.

NORMAN. Shouldn't we remove our make-up, Sir?

(SIR *stares at himself in the looking-glass*)

SIR. I shall leave nothing. Nothing. (*Pause*) I hope Will's pleased tonight.

NORMAN. I had a friend—

SIR. Oh for Christ's sake, I'm sick of your friends.

Motley crew they are. Pathetic, lonely, despairing—

NORMAN. That's nice, isn't it?

SIR. I beg your pardon. Uncalled for. Count myself as your friend.

NORMAN. Never despairing

SIR. Have apologised.

NORMAN. Never, never despairing. Well. Perhaps. Sometimes. At night. Or at Christmas when you can't get a pantomime. But not once inside the building. Never. Pathetic maybe, but not ungrateful. Too mindful of one's luck, as the saying goes. No duke is more privileged. Here's beauty. Here's spring and summer. Here pain is bearable. And never lonely. Not here. For he today that sheds his blood with me. Soft, no doubt. Sensitive. That's my nautre. Easily hurt but that's a virtue. I'm not here for reasons of my own either. No one could accuse me of base motives. I've got what I want and I don't need anyone to know it. Inadequate, yes. But never, never despairing.

(HER LADYSHIP *enters dressed in her own clothes*)

HER LADYSHIP. Not started to change yet?

SIR. I'm a little slow tonight, Pussy.

HER LADYSHIP. I'm not waiting. I'll go back to the digs, see if I can get a fire lit.

SIR. I shan't be long.

HER LADYSHIP. Goodnight, Norman. I'm not certain whether I should thank you or not.

NORMAN. Not. I can't bear being thanked.

(SHE *goes*)

SIR. A good woman. (SIR *applies cold cream slowly and wearily and when the mask is covered and the colours a blur,* HE *lets out a sudden moan and cannot apparently move*)

NORMAN. Sir, what is it, Sir?

(SIR *moans*)

SIR. I'm—I'm tired. Terribly tired. The room is spinning. I—I must lie down

(NORMAN *quickly helps him to the couch.* SIR *lies back*)

SIR. See if you can get me a taxi in this Godforsaken place.

NORMAN. All in good time. (*No response.* NORMAN *takes cotton wool and begins to clean* SIR's *face.* SIR *begins to cry*) Don't cry. Don't cry.

SIR. There's nothing left.

NORMAN Stop that at once.

SIR. I've begun *My Life.*

NORMAN. What?

SIR. Fetch it. The book. I made a start—

(NORMAN *brings it to him*)

SIR. Find the place.

(NORMAN *pages through the book*)

NORMAN. You didn't get very far—

SIR. What did I write?

NORMAN. (HE *reads*) My Life. Dedication. This book is dedicated to My Beloved Pussy who has been my splended spur. To the spirit of all actors because of their faith and endurance which never fails them. To Those who do the work of the theatre yet have but small share in its glory: Carpenters, Electricians, Scene-shifters, Property men. To the Audiences who have laughed with us, have wept with us and whose hearts have united with ours in sympathy and understanding. And finally—ah Sir— to the memory of William Shakespeare in whose glorious service we all labour.

(*Silence*)

SIR. *My Life* will have to do.

(*Silence*)

NORMAN. Wait a moment, wait a moment—(HE *re-reads the passage*) "Carpenters, electricians, pro-perty-men . . ." But Sir, Sir—(NORMAN *looks at him*) Sir? Sir? (HE *shakes* SIR *gently. A long pause*) We're not dead are we? (*Silence. For the first time* NORMAN's *drunkenness shows physically.* HE *staggers, almost falls*—) You're right. The room is spinning. (HE *regains his balance, stands staring at* SIR, *then is seized by terror and panic.* HE *stumbles, to the door*—) Your ladyship! Madge! Anybody! (HE *stands in the doorway, whimpering.* MADGE *hurries into the corridor, then past him into the dressing room.* NORMAN *takes a step inside and watches her.* MADGE *looks down at* SIR. SHE *is perfectly*

still. SHE *lets out a soft short cry but then controls
herself. Silence)* Wasn't much of a death scene. Un-
remarkable and ever so short. For him.

(MADGE *turns away from the* BODY)

MADGE. Where's Her Ladyship?
NORMAN. Left before he did. Couldn't wait.
MADGE. I'll get a doctor.
NORMAN. Too late for a doctor, ducky.

(MADGE *takes* SIR's *Lear cloak and covers the* BODY
with it)

NORMAN. What's to happen to me?
MADGE. Close the door. Wait outside.
NORMAN. You're nothing now, ducky. He took away
your stripes. And mine. How could he be so bloody
careless?
MADGE. Come away.
NORMAN. And then where will I go? Where?
I'm nowhere out of my element. I don't want to
end up running a boarding house in Westcliff-on-Sea.
Or Colwyn Bay. What am I going to do?
MADGE. You can speak well of him.
NORMAN. Speak well of that old sod? I wouldn't
give him a good character, not in a court of law.
Ungrateful bastard. Silence, ducky. My lips are sealed.
MADGE. Get out. I don't want you in here.
NORMAN. Holy, holy, holy, is it? Are we in a
shrine? No pissing on the altar—
MADGE. Stop it.
NORMAN. He never once took me out for a meal.

Never once. Always a back seat, me. Can't even remember him buying me a drink. And just walks out, leaves me, no thought for anyone but himself. What have I been doing here all these years? Why? (HE *turns away from her*) Speak well of him? I know what you'd say, ducky. I know all about you. I've got eyes in my head. We all have our little sorrows. (MADGE *goes but* NORMAN *does not notice*) I know what you'd say, stiff upper, faithful, loyal. Loving. Well, I have only one thing to say about him and I wouldn't say it in front of you—or Her Ladyship, or anyone. Lips tight shut. I wouldn't give you the pleasure. Or him. Specially not him. If I said what I have to say he' d find a way to take it out on me. No one will ever know. We all have our little sorrows, ducky, you're not the only one. The littler you are, the larger the sorrow. You think *you* loved him? What about me? (*Long silence*) This is not a place for death. I had a friend—(HE *turns suddenly as if aware of someone behind him, but realises* HE *is alone*) Sir? Sir? (*Silence.* HE *hugs the exercise book.* HE *sings*—) "He that has a little tiny wit, With hey, ho, the wind and the rain." (HE *falls silent.* HE *stares into space, Lights fade.*)

THE END

SET NOTES

FLOOR

Off Stage Area: Old concrete, dirty with areas of paint, spill Arditex or similar light-weight texture applied on top of ply.

Wing Space Area: Heavily textured wooden planks with part-stencils stuck to floor. Spilled paint, walked in. 3"x5/8" hardwood boards. Planks have originally been varnished, but many layers of dirt have been ground in and varnish has been worn off. Areas patched where incendiary devices have come through the ceiling, but nevertheless showing scorched and burn areas. Plaster has come down from the ceiling in places and has been walked into the floor. Three stage dips, cast iron with design relief in the top are let into the floor, flush with the boarding surface. Cables are then running out of these into the perch positions (these need not be practical).

On Stage Area: Stage cloth cracked with over painting, torn and patched. Has marks of previous shows (flat positions) roughly marked in; should be tacked down on on-stage edge, very untidily. Should have remnant of flag stones painted in from previous show, but this has been mostly rubbed out.

Dressing Room Floor: Must look as if they're old boards. Edge has been painted with dark oak lacquer where original carpet has ended. This carpet now no longer exists and has been replaced by a smaller one from the prop room, leaving bare, dirty boarding exposed, which the original carpeting would have covered.

Corridor: Covered in old, thick brown linoleum, which has been nailed down in places where continual use has broken and split it; in some places, the hessian base is showing through. There is a white line painted on the entrance to the stage area; again, everything should be rotting and dirty.

Steps: Three dimensional bricks, layed in pattern, painted, and then grouted. Bricks not to be new, but old and crumbly, edges worn down through constant use. Surface must not deteriorate through actors' use.

L. X. Gallery: Scaffolding boards, black under with practical working light; plaster walked into floor.

Fly Floor: Scaffolding board, black under with practical working light; plaster walked into floor.

WALLS

Off Stage: Three dimensional bricks, applied to 1/4" ply; mortar coming out in sections; bricks to be old. On stage buttress to have double-skin; outer skin cut through in sections, particularly down-stage corner to allow the visual effect of a broken corner; bricks missing, ruined masonry, yet retaining solidity as an inner core of bricks is revealed. This is boxed unit which is then attached to the other flatage. Girders to be timber but to look like rusty steel; exits under to the scenic paint shop; walls will have brush marks where brushes have been cleaned. Pipes above slop sink should have many layers of scenic paint; sink to be filthy. Fire hoses, very heavy. They, therefore, need steel bracing but must look as if it is bolted straight into the brick wall. All water pipes are not practical. Old scenery, broken and tatty, is stacked against the up-stage edge of the o.p. corner, where corridor is to allow masked entrance to the dressing room.

Corridor Back Wall: Arditex, or similar light plaster equivalent texture stenciled on ply up to 1/4" in thickness, 1/2" if possible, to look like old bricks, not new. Brick color to be painted over all surfaces and then over-painted in blue, as model. Blue to be badly applied in sections to reveal brick color under. Lamp brackets: cast iron and filigreed. All piping needs to be supplied, plus the hand rail up the steps. Softboard notice board, framed in timber, dirty, many pin marks and regulation notices, war news, etc., pinned on. Window: steel-barred. Several glass panes broken, patched with cardboard and paper, very filthy and crisscrossed with brown paper and gum strip; also need a good fixing for the English coin telephone required.

Wing Space, Gallery Wall: Three dimensional bricks, textured, painted and then grouted; up to 2" thicknessing sections are then applied on top of this to resemble real plaster. This area must look as if through bomb-blast, the plaster has come down; so, in color, you would have red brick, the grey-yellow of the mortar, white-grey edge of the plaster, blue surface of the paint, plus the graffiti on top of that.

Dressing Room: Half-plaster and wainscotting; plaster down in places, revealing lathing and space behind. Water pipes above should be lagged, very old, dirty, rust marks showing. All walls need to be very rigid; door slammed and knocked. If any vibration occurs on pipes above or in walls, illusion will be destroyed. Old water tank above with water pipes. Not practical, but pipes extending into the space above. Tank should be zinc. Door needs Victorian glass, frosted with clear pattern, crisscrossed with gum strip because of the bomb blast. Cracked in places. Old brass door handles with box lock. Door knocker and brass name plate, worn letters, no distinguishable name. Wainscotting behind the sink, green with water mold, very dirty.

STEEL FLY FLOOR UNIT

Metal fluted upright painted in gloss paint many, many times showing layers of paint, now has been left for years so the gloss has been dulled and paint has chipped to steel. Wooden ladder has been originally varnished, some aging process has occurred, center of rungs worn down to curve and varnish worn off where hands have been. Steel construction ought to have undergone a similar aging process.

FLATAGE

Old flats from previous shows, all creased and lined, but in this case, battened together roughly. Flats marked PS 1 and so forth. Names of previous shows (i.e. HAMLET) scrubbed out and overpainted with LEAR, but still showing through. Tormentors lined with old canvas, but appears to be fronted with wine red velour, which has been untidily wrapped around the edge and tacked. Reveal piece on tormentor border. Stage braces should be a steel rod with hook and are not adjustable. Cleat lines and canvas must look 20 years old.

PRACTICALS AND FLYING PIECES

Dressing Room: One inch conduit frame. One practical lamp extending into corridor area. Flown on two downstage positions on thinnest wire possible. Dirty cream, very dusty. The upstage edge should be attached to the cupboard and the lighting gallery. May need an inner core steel to stop bowing. Must be rigid and not buckle.

Dressing Table: 3/4" conduit frame, four working bulbs and a two-way mirror.

Sink: Practical tap and drainage.

Gas Ring: Needs to be practical and boils a kettle.

Center Lamp: Cord must be material covered, not plastic.

Gas Mantles: Two are required, electrified to look like gas.

Corridor: 1 lamp over stair: other is a dud bulb.

Gas Mantles: 1 is required, electrified to look like gas.

L. X. and Fly Floor Unit: Iron release handle, needs to be pulled by an actor, sprung so it returns to its original position; needs to clank or hit on ratchet. NOISY.

Front Curtain: Pully; this is worked by an actor. Hemp rope with deadlines marked. Just a continual loop.

Panatrope: (78 Record Player) Turntable to turn and bulbs in side amplified to work. Worked by an actor and cued.

Cue Lights: Small boxes with red and green independents, worked by actor from cue switches mounted on stage management desk; these should be brass. Desk should also have angle poise.

Dimmer: Old, sliding resistance dimmer with mounted blue bulb on top; required to be worked by actor.

Plaster Bag: Released in a bomb-blast. Should be old, gilded plaster from stucco ceiling plus a lot of light dust; not many large pieces.

Other working machinery includes: Wind machine; Rain machine; Thunder sheet; Set of tymps; Grand master handles working not electrified.

COSTUME PLOT

SIR
Dark blue suit
Black lace-up shoes
Overcoat
Towelling Dressing gown
Underwear
Silk/wool Lear tunic
Lear cloak
Crown
Belt
Second Lear cloak & brooch

NORMAN
Polo-neck shirt
Black trousers
Pumps

HER LADYSHIP
Scarlet dressing gown
Coronet & veil
White shift
Gas-mask case

MADGE
Brown cord coat
Blue wool dress

Hat
Black crepe dress
Gas-mask case

GEOFFREY THORNTON
Corduroy suit
Grey slip-over
Broad-brimmed felt hat
Burberry
Brown brogues
Metal helmet
Gas-mask case

MR. OXENBY
Edmund tunic
Gauntlets
Belt & sword
Black lace-up boots with caliper
Long black boots
Tweed jacket
Grey flannels
Slip-over
Burberry
Gas-mask case

LEAR'S KNIGHTS
Knitted armour
3 metal helmets
4 cloaks
4 tunics
2 circlets
Sword & sword-belt

FURNITURE LIST

Skip
Dressing table
Swivel chair
Armchair
2 chairs
Chaise
Round table
Basin
Radiator
Table with gas ring
Stool
Rain machine
Wind machine
Panatrope
Prompt desk
Tympani
Stool
Cleat rail

PROP LIST

ACT I

¼ bottle brandy
Tea caddy
Jam jar of sugar
Milk in ½ pt. bottle
3+ mugs
Biscuit tin & biscuits (very thin)
Small teapot
Wig block
Matches
Small box for beard & moustache
Tea strainer
Kettle
Silver make-up tray
Make-up
Towel (to cover tray)
Cigarette box & cigarettes
Ashtray
White runner for dressing table
Spirit gum & surgical spirit
Brushes
Bowl
Packet of 'Brown & Poulsons'
Powder puff & brush
Tin of removing cream
Meat paste jar for mixing glue
Cotton wool (interleaved with blue paper)
Comb

Broken spectacles (in soft case) 1 lens smashed,
  1 cracked
Exercise book
Waste paper basket
Triple crown
Soap
Notebook
Towels
Bar of chocolate
Jewellery box & jewels
Ring
Map
Mirror—magnifying & plain on a stand

ACT II

Whip
Script of "Lear" (Temple edition)
Rug
Chamois leather
Return (in envelope)
Sewing bag & tights
Prompt copy
Photos of Sir
Tray
Glasses
2 1/4 bottles brandy
Pint bottle beer
Bottle scotch
Beer mug
Manuscript of Oxenby's play
Brandy
Pencil
Tin hat

Cash box & key
Records
Pint of stout
2 shoe horns—1 small, 1 very large
Saucer
Hair brush
Clothes brush
Polishing cloth
Cushion on chaise
Small tray
Powder puff
Soap rack to hang in sink

SPECIAL EFFECTS

SINK:
   Running cold H_2O & drainage

GAS RING:
   Lit w/match
   Boils kettle of H_2O
   Must have "Off " handle

GAS MANTLES:
   3 practical

PLASTER DROP BOX:
   Shop to provide box
   Elec. Release
   Need plaster

Thunder sheet
Wind machine
Rain machine